T0128964

My Pen in the Hands of the Lord

Milagros Arzola

authorHOUSE®

AuthorHouse™
1663 Liberty Drive
Bloomington, IN 47403
www.authorhouse.com
Phone: 833-262-8899

Published by AuthorHouse 05/21/2021

ISBN: 978-1-6655-2705-7 (sc)
ISBN: 978-1-6655-2704-0 (e)

Library of Congress Control Number: 2021910502

Print information available on the last page.

This book is printed on acid-free paper.

Milagros Arzola lives in Florida with her husband, with whom she has been married for 46 years. She studied her Bachelor of the Arts at the University of Puerto Rico and her master's at Lesley College in Cambridge, Massachusetts. She is currently an active member of a Christian church in the state of Florida, where both she and her husband are leaders of the congregation.

Contents

Preface

My Pen in the Hands of the Lord has the goal of conveying my intimate desire to transmit a positive message that nurtures all of my fellow humans in need. This collection of poems is also a song of praise for the Creator. It contains the praise and inspiration that God has given me when I have asked for them in prayer.

I am certain, dear reader, that you will find nourishment for your soul when you read these poems inspired by God. He is the purveyor of our talents, which he gives to his children when they ask for them from their heart, in order to honor him as he deserves. I hope you enjoy this book and take relish in God with each poem.

It is dedicated to you, with much affection.

Milagros Arzola

My Pen in the Hands of the Lord

My pen is in your hands, my Lord,
for you to use to trace, dear Lord,
thoughts most beautiful, thoughts most human,
to exalt your greatness, my dear Lord.

My pen is in your hands, my Lord,
to tell of you and lovingly express
the deep love of the words of my hand
which to you, dear Savior, I direct.

My pen is in your hands, my Lord,
to be used for your honor and your glory,
pouring out all you would have me express,
my Jesus, through the pages of my story.

Drop by Drop

Drop by drop dripped your blood,
dear Lord, trickling down a cross,
gifting me through your precious nectar
salvation and eternal life with your loss.

Drop by drop on the cross, dear Lord,
down dripped the stains of your love,
consummating your work of redemption
to save my soul with your blood.

Of your actions I am not worthy
and of the drops of your blood even less,
your sacrifice goes far beyond me,
but you sacrificed yourself nonetheless.

For this, dear Lord, let me offer
my life to you, now, drop by drop.
I am yours for you to use my talents
for your glory, as that is their job.

You Take Control

Alongside my Christ, crucified I am,
I live no more—but Christ lives in me;
no longer following the whims that come knocking,
but the will of the Savior who lives inside me.

When in vain my pride tries to overcome me,
threatening to wound another of my kind,
all it takes is a glance toward the crucifix
to put out the pride corrupting my mind.

When feelings of meanness try to seep in,
my shortsighted ego may give them room,
but you gave your everything, in return for
nothing,
so my greatest desire is to give my life to you.

When my rage threatens to let out my anger,
I remember Moses, as he struck the rock.
You ordered him to speak, but he struck with
rage,
and his pass to the Promised Land then he lost.

For my flesh, to you, I hand myself over,
eternal celestial potter, for you to conduce
control of my existence, I deliver my spirit
to you as an instrument for you to use.

The Peace Provided by Christ

The peace that you provide, my Christ,
I cannot receive it from the world;
from you alone it comes, with love
to mankind, feelings of peace unfurled.

My spirit lies in you, my Lord.
So perfect and sublime is your peace!
Nothing surpasses its intensity,
as immense as he who bestowed it on me.

Nothing, my Lord, will I allow to disturb
your loving peace, so full of pleasure.
My untiring spirit, saying its prayers
keeps watch over this unparalleled treasure.

My Refuge

Dear Lord, you have been my refuge
from the very first day that we met.
Not in vain you became part of my life;
to you, all my happiness, I owe in debt.

The night terrors that would come upon me,
phantoms harassing me from all sides,
while the past is home to my fantasies,
in the present, you, my King, reside.

Lord, you have taken away my worries,
the confusion of my mind now a past thing felt.
My burdens today I place in your hands,
to never again take upon myself.

Dear Lord, oh how marvelous you are!
You are guide and support in this world.
With you my life is nothing but beauty,
and in you I rest, as I know I should.

Love for God

The melodious chirping of birds in the trees
could never be enough to put into words
the great love burning for you in my bosom
which to you, dear Lord, I humbly confer.

Waterfalls great that you have created,
the beauty of the sound as downward they fall:
they do not come close to conveying my feelings;
they cannot explain the magnitude of it all.

The sun beaming down with the warmth that it
gifts us,
surrounding us all in its thousands of rays,
can never come close to the sublime love I feel
for you, my Lord, a love so great!

The moon and the thousand romances it inspires,
humans in love, man singing in delight;
it might not understand the burning inside me,
this storm-like flame that in me you light.

You are praised by the birds in their chirping,
and nature is here to tell us of your splendor,
but all that my vehement heart can express now
is the immensely deep love which to you I
surrender.

No More Pain

In a desert of semi-lit darkness
at the height of my affliction
when I felt most distant from you, my Lord,
I lifted my eyes to the sky and exclaimed,
in desperation:
open the doors of my cell
get me out of this prison.
No more pain, no more pain, dear Lord.
Save me by saying your name!
Hear my prayer
lift me and with your power I will sing,
O, strength of mine, Lord of my salvation.

All I ask is love for those people
who have hurt me, my Lord, and who I never
paid
with pain, with my pain...
I left my pain on the cross
and on the cross it will remain
as the cross can be only a symbol of love and
pardon.

Divine Lamb

You are a worthy lamb, immaculate;
you offered to die on the cross for me.
for me you stayed silent, for me you were judged,
and later condemned to a death so mean.

Worthy, you are, O dignified lamb,
sacrificed by all of humanity.
What a noble sacrifice of greatness
of he who lived his life in sanctity.

And undeserving, your body beaten
without a word, withstanding it for me,
O precious lamb.

Worthy you are, my lamb,
your precious blood you gave
to wipe away the sins of humanity.
You are the bread of life, of eternal life:
the perfect offering for the salvation of the world.

Isaiah 53

Scorned and disregarded, you went to the cross,
O Lord,
son of pains, experienced in
sorrows.
We hid our faces from you, we thought less of you,
we did not appreciate you: we hurt you, we
wounded you...

But you, wounded, went, for our rebellions;
But you, weakened, went, for our sins.
The punishment for our peace fell upon you, O
Lord
Jesus,
and through your wounds, dear Jesus, we were
cured.

You were delivered to your death, your blood
the cross stained,
and for our sinfulness, you were humiliated, O
Lord.
And we, full of fear, abandoned you on the cross,
leaving you behind in the midst of your pain.

Open Book

My Lord, I'm like an open book for you to read,
because you know everything—everything about
me.
You know of my shortcomings and of my
weaknesses;
you know all that which I cannot yet perceive.

Because you know everything—everything about
me,
my Lord, I'm like an open book for you to read.
You know the steps of my life, my comings
and goings,
and all of it you scrutinize, O omnipotent Lord!

Your spirit reads, deep down inside me,
and chastens me for my human condition.
What of my life, if it weren't for your love?
What of me, if it weren't for your direction?

Because you know everything—everything about
me,
my Lord, I'm like an open book for you to read.
Where can I go, if to hide from you I flee?
If I go up to heaven you will be there,
and if I hide in the oceans, you will know where.
Because you know everything—everything about
me,
my Lord, I'm an open book for you to read.

The Tempest

The twelve apostles went a-sailing,
sailing along in a boat
over to the other bank of the river,
doing as good Jesus told.

Suddenly a wind of great fury
against them unleashed its shear,
as the boat that held them trembled
and flooded their hearts with fear.

Whipped around by the waves
and stranded in the middle of the sea,
the boat on the verge of going under,
with danger so very near.

But as the fourth watch drew closer
during that dark, fearful night,
Jesus came to visit to the vessel,
over the water walking upright.

Seeing him walk over the water
the men wondered with confusion
if he were no more than a phantom,
a shape before their eyes, an illusion.

And voices of fear could be heard,
but Jesus calmed them with his words:
"Do not fear; see, I am here."
And Peter then spoke in return:
"If that is you, my Savior,
I would also walk on water."

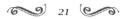

"Come," the good master spoke to him
and Peter stepped out of the boat,
walking on top of the water,
to return to his Jesus, our Lord.

But when he saw the wind's power
from Christ he removed his gaze,
hence fear overcame poor Peter,
and soon enough he was sinking away.

"Save me, oh Lord!" shouted Peter,
now overcome with despair,
so Jesus held his outstretched hand,
ready to help he was there.

But then Jesus gave him harsh words,
for ever coming to doubt,
for letting his gaze stray away,
and for allowing his fear to sprout.

Often, we, the believers,
when lost in the sea of affliction,
we do the same thing as Peter,
and doubt he who brings us salvation.

We take our gaze off of the Lord,
we no longer look at him straight,
we no longer open our arms to him,
while he to receive us always awaits.

As prisoners of fear we are doubtful,
losing ourselves in the trial,
while he is always there, desirous,
waiting for you with a smile.

Repose in Christ and wait,
and soon you will see victory,
because what is faith but certainty
of what is not yet but soon will be.

I Give Myself to You

I give myself to you, Lord, in a song,
a sublime melody of an offering,
gifted to you.
Celestial notes of your inspiration, my Lord,
flowing like a river through my being,
inscribed lovingly on a sheet of paper.

My Lord, you are deserving of melodies,
the most beautiful that could ever exist,
the purest feelings
a human being could express
honoring and exalting you alone.

The Coming of the Son of God

The son of God will come,
like a clever thief in the dark,
causing great surprise in this world,
the coming of the son of God.

For some people it is just fiction,
for others fable it seems,
keeping vigil deep in their hearts,
with his name their souls to redeem.

The signs that he left behind,
symbols to mark his return,
not a single one remains lacking,
all have now been affirmed.

And of all of these heavenly signs
left behind by our Lord, the Savior,
one of them stands out among others
as an hourglass for all our behavior.

He said: "Learn a parable of the fig tree;
when his branch is yet tender,
and putteth forth leaves,
ye know that summer is nigh."

And now that the fig tree has flowered,
we know that summer is here,
and soon he for whom we await
will come and before us appear.

And in case you didn't know it,
the fig tree is Israel,
once again back to its origin,
and fulfilled all of the signals.

Just as God has promised,
planting them with firm feet,
sowing them in the lands that are his,
and they flowered unlimitedly.

Like You

Like you, unparalleled,
because you fill my soul with peace
turning my torments to calm.

Like you, unparalleled,
your love washes away my sins
as your blood pours out on the Cavalry.

Who would pay for my sins as you have?
Who would give their life for me as you have?
Who would shed their blood as you have?
Drop by drop for love!

Only you—you who are unparalleled
with your inconceivable love.
Only you—you who are unparalleled
with your love for human kind.

The Word

In the beginning was the Word,
and the Word was with God,
and the Word was God;
Through him all things were made;
without him nothing was made
that has been made.

And the Word became flesh
and dwelt among us,
and the Word came to the world,
which did not know it,
but those that accepted it were
called the children of God
and that Word turned flesh loved them;
in the beginning was the Word.

And this Word, dear friend,
this Word is my Jesus.
And this Word, dear friend,
is the world of light,
which lovingly offers the gift of salvation,
do not reject his loving invitation;
in the beginning was the Word.

I Give Thanks

Thank you, my Lord, for this new day,
as now I can see the dawn of a new morning.
You in your infinite love have allowed me
to enjoy to the utmost, I thank you my King.

I thank you for the chirping of the birds,
never ceasing as the morning's
rays shine through,
this exquisite banquet that to me you offer
and which I enjoy with the
peace bestowed by you.

I thank you for the light entering my eyes,
the majestic and beautiful
sunlight shining through,
tenderly caressing me in the midst of its rays,
with the tenderness infused into them by you.

I thank you for the air that I breathe
from the very moment at which I was born.
Thank you, my Lord, as you live within me,
and I live because you inside me take on form.

Thank you, O Lord, for the
chance to have met you,
for living in communion together as one.
Dear Lord, my pleasure is far past description,
my God, to you alone my heart belongs.

Divine Love

Would that I could extend the wings
of my enamored soul
and reach out to you, God eternal
and in your presence remain;
would that I could be with you already,
taking pleasure in your presence,
contemplating your beauty,
and your unsurpassable charm.

O Great Man of Galilee!
Your indescribable beauty
already tempts my eyes
with utmost longing;
would that I could see the splendor
of the brilliant light
shining forth from your being
like a lightning strike never-ending.

I have no greater burning desire
than to extend my wings
and soar up toward your presence
in sublime adoration
eternally embracing
contemplating your beauty
and enjoying forever after
your unparalleled love.

To My Daughter

My girl, don't let life knock you down,
don't let the pain confuse you or lose you,
my girl, life is short, before you know it's gone,
and after the storm the calm will always ensue.

And if at some time, pain
shows up at your door,
time will be the cure of all of your worries.
If, before you, a new disappointment unfolds,
there is always an opportunity
inside that it carries.

This life brings new surprises every day,
happiness, sadness, moments of disgrace.
But my girl, after the dark night fades away,
a beautiful morning will
unfold before your face.

That's just life, how things are, my girl,
bit by bit, precautious, you sip away
at this life more priceless than any gold or jewel,
put in to your hands by God every day.

To My Mother

The word "mother" holds in it
the unparalleled delight
that every mother gives her little one
in unsurpassable self-sacrifice.

Mother in all tongues
means love in all of its power;
mother, you are the sweet scent
arising from the beautiful flower.

From your chalice and its nectar
God's miracle comes forth,
there I was created, dear mother,
from you, source of my birth.

Death at the birth of another
ill-fated and cruel looked in store
but you cried out to heaven, O mother,
for a miracle by hand of our Lord.

Your arms, enveloped in sobs,
you raised them to Heaven in prayer
seizing a miracle from God
who for your affliction offered care.

God is kind, O mother of mine.
As we know, he answered your pleas,
and today, at this very moment in time,
I praise him for his kindly mercy.

And God, his miracle completed,
granted with his open arms,
salvation in all of its glory,
to both of our humanly forms.

And now, today, united,
we praise God hand-in-hand,
our love all the more perfect
if we live for God so grand.

Your Strength

Your strength accompanies me day to day,
helping me travel the steps on my path;
a fight turning more arduous along the way
in which my own strength is not always enough.

A new battle awaits me ahead, eternal King.
The armies of hell attack me ever stronger
every day that I look out over a new morning
and I need your help to emerge the victor.

How good it is, my Lord, to
live under your wing!
How good it is to know you are here to assist!
My soul holds strong when you are here for me;
if you fight by my side, I will resist!

At the sound of the trumpet, triumphant I call
the battle is over, my fight come to an end,
but the greatest reward, as I bid farewell,
will be seeing you in your Glory up in heaven!

I seek no crowns, no riches, no praise,
only in the bounty of your love to delight,
only upon the glory of your beauty to gaze,
your greatness to extol and your
splendor appreciate.

The Great I Am

Let all languages state
that you alone are our Lord,
and all knees shall bend
before the Saint of Israel.
Because you are Excelsior King,
you are the beginning and the end,
Lord, we exalt you and adore you:
You are the Great I Am!

All nations shall adore you,
O dear Saint of Israel!
Glory and honor in entirety
belong to you alone.
Because you are the Great I Am,
so tall and sublime that you are.
For that all peoples shall honor you
and all knees shall bend
to adore the Great I Am!

Despite the Storm

You keep me safe despite the storm, my Christ,
You are my eternal refuge, my anchor, my light,
and in the middle of my trials, your
ineffable peace invades me,
what a pleasure to serve You,
my dearly loved Lord!

Care for my life, God, care for my heart;
may my soul never be afflicted by evil
if You, dear Jesus, are always on my mind,
flooding my being with your presence, my Lord.

You accompany me despite
the storm, my Christ.
Carrying me in your arms,
my burdens you bear,
and if you are always with me,
I have nothing to fear.
In the middle of my trials, your
promises I will remember
because I know that you are
faithful, my Jesus so dear.

I Praise You, My Lord

I praise you with all of my soul, my Lord,
with all of my being and reasoning too,
I praise you with my innards,
with all of my senses;
oh how glorious and sublime is your love!

Oh how great is your mercy!
How saintly and perfect your love!
You took mankind out of the void
bestowing on our life a great wealth!

You transformed our cries into dances
with unparalleled pleasure, my Lord
giving a new direction to we humans
placing a new song on our lips.

For this, of you, I speak glory.
I never tire of praising my great God;
so long as I live I will praise you,
receive my praise, O my Creator.

Traveler

Traveler moving along walking
along the road to Canaan
a long way yet lies ahead
for you to travel along.
At times you will be tempted
to turn your back on the path,
but if you leave behind Christ
victory you shall never have.

The path ahead is not easy,
many obstacles lie in wait,
but ever greater the reward
that he will give the end.
Traveler, there is much danger
in straying your gaze to the side,
but always there will be honor
if with firm footing you arrive.
As long ago, the rays of the dawn
Lot's wife saw from behind
and for her disobeying
she was made into a statue of salt.

Printed in the United States
by Baker & Taylor Publisher Services